100 Reasons
To
Hate Trump

ISBN: 9781798776254

Because He Is Trump

Because He Is Republican

Because He Is Not A Democrat

Because He Is Not A Libertarian

Because He Is Not Green Party

Because He Is White

Because He Is Not Black

Because He Is Not Spanish

Because He Is Not Asian

Because He Is A Man

Because He Is Not A Woman

Because He Is Angry

Because He Is Not Passive

Because He Is Vulgar

Because He Is Uncouth

Because He Is Rude

Because He Is Lewd

Because He Is Rude

Because He Is Crass

Because He Is Disgusting

Because He Is Red

Because He Is Not Blue

Because He Is Odd

Because He Is A Racist

Because He Is Opinionated

Because He Is Tyrannical

Because He Is Harsh

Because He Is Depressing

Because He Is Overpowering

Because He Is Tacky

Because He Is Terrible

Because He Is Toxic

Because He Is Venomous

Because He Is Dirty

Because He Is Crude

Because He Is Bad

Because He Is Outlandish

Because He Is Nasty

Because He Is Straight

Because He Is Not Gay

Because He Is Not Transgender

Because He Is Not Androgynous

Because He Is Not Bisexual

Because He Is Not Gender-Fluid

Because He Is Not Non-Binary

Because He Is Arrogant

Because He Is Not Humble

Because He Is Not Kind

Because He Is Overconfident

Because He Is Self-Important

Because He Is Egotistical

Because He Is Narcissistic

Because He Is Vain

Because He Is Self-Absorbed

Because He Is Not Selfless

Because He is a Isolationist

Because He is Not Obama

Because He is Not Hillary

Because He has Orange Hair

Because He was Divorced

Because He Is Pathetic

Because He Is Pitiful

Because He Is Laughable

Because He Is A Pervert

Because He Is Absurd

Because He Is Useless

Because He Is Stupid

Because He Is Absurd

Because He Is Laughable

Because He Is Obtuse

Because He Is Asinine

Because He Is Dangerous

Because He Is Shady

Because He Is Dishonest

Because He Is Crooked

Because He Is Devious

Because He Is Deceitful

Because He Is Untrustworthy

Because He Is Fake

Because He Is Phony

Because He Is Fanatical

Because He Is Presbyterian

Because He Is Not Jewish

Because He Is Not Muslim

Because He Is Not Buddhist

Because He Is Not Mormon

Because He Is Not Hindu

Because He Is Not Atheist

Because He Is Not Wiccan

Because He Is Not Baptist

Because He Is Not Lutheran

Because He Is Not Taoist

Because He Is Despicable

Because He Is Shameful

Because He Is Not Nice

Because He Is Horrible

Because He Is Upsetting

Because America

Because You Can

Because He Is still Trump

www.ingramcontent.com/pod-product-compliance
Lightning Source LLC
Chambersburg PA
CBHW030357280726

48655CB00019B/2305